SIMPLE MODERN
SRI LANKAN
Cooking
WITH
MAHESHA RICE
(Founder of Rice's Bliss)

Dear Customer,

Sri Lankan kitchens are the heart of the home. As I relive my childhood memories, I am transported back to our family kitchen, with its jars of spices filling shelves and the sound of freshly picked herbs being ground, their aroma filling the house. Weekends brought a lively buzz of activity, with my sisters and I gathering fresh curry leaves, and my mum managing many bubbling pans. Bowlfuls of rice and curry were laid on the table to share with friends. Ensuring guests are comfortable is central to Sri Lankan hosting, and so my mum would stay in the kitchen, prepping the many dishes until the final morsels were left to show our guests were full. This devotion, care and attention formed our cultural narrative, and a tradition I love to share.

Doors to Sri Lankan houses are always open, friends are welcomed and family are loved. Everyone is fed, and no one leaves with an empty stomach. As you recreate my recipes in your home, I hope you combine your own traditions with mine, and enjoy sharing delicious, wholesome food with your loved ones.

Remember, for even more ideas for family-friendly meals, head over to RicesBliss.com website.

Happy Cooking,

Mahesha Rice
RICE'S BLISS

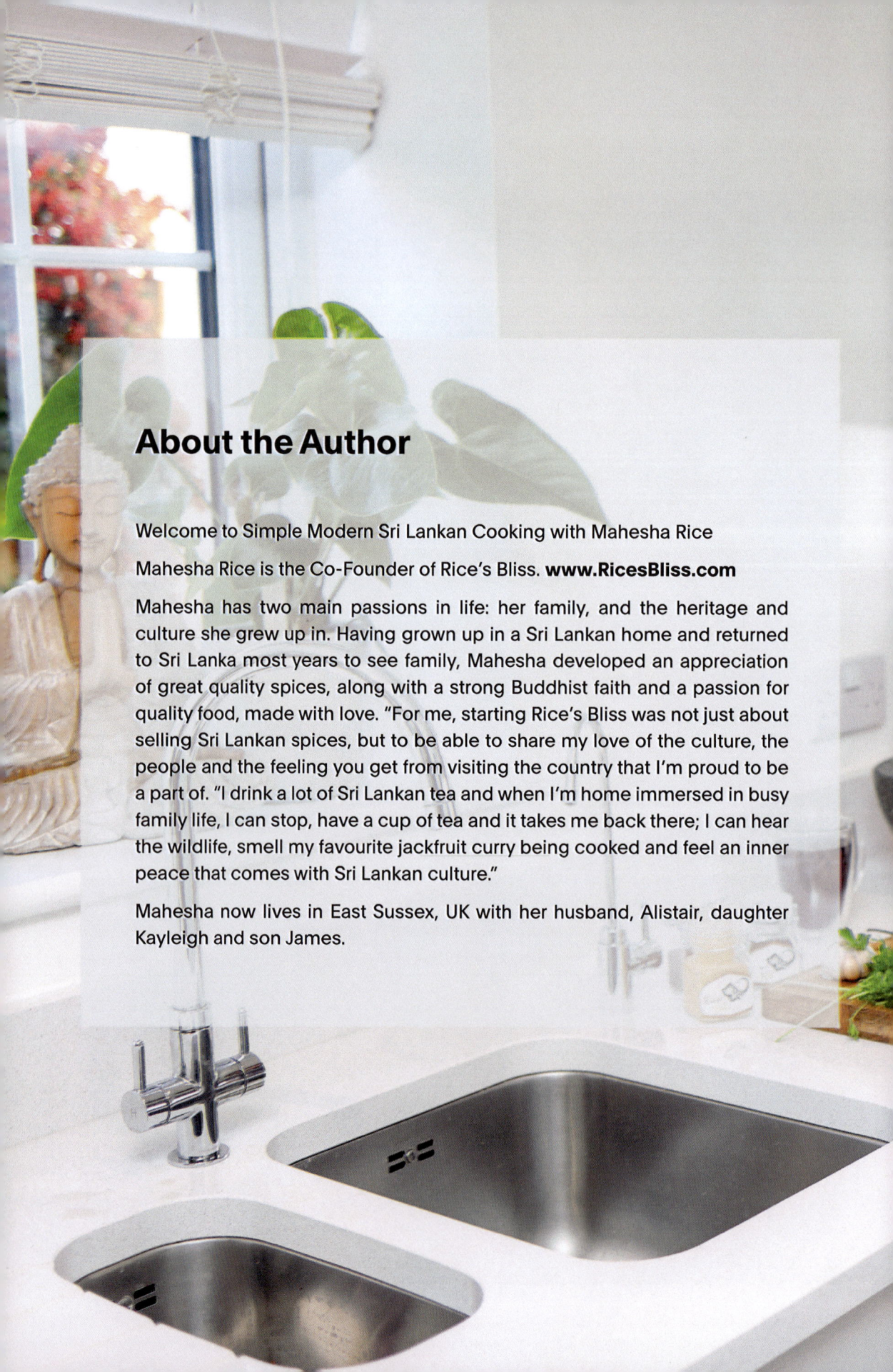

About the Author

Welcome to Simple Modern Sri Lankan Cooking with Mahesha Rice

Mahesha Rice is the Co-Founder of Rice's Bliss. **www.RicesBliss.com**

Mahesha has two main passions in life: her family, and the heritage and culture she grew up in. Having grown up in a Sri Lankan home and returned to Sri Lanka most years to see family, Mahesha developed an appreciation of great quality spices, along with a strong Buddhist faith and a passion for quality food, made with love. "For me, starting Rice's Bliss was not just about selling Sri Lankan spices, but to be able to share my love of the culture, the people and the feeling you get from visiting the country that I'm proud to be a part of. "I drink a lot of Sri Lankan tea and when I'm home immersed in busy family life, I can stop, have a cup of tea and it takes me back there; I can hear the wildlife, smell my favourite jackfruit curry being cooked and feel an inner peace that comes with Sri Lankan culture."

Mahesha now lives in East Sussex, UK with her husband, Alistair, daughter Kayleigh and son James.

The Story behind Rice's Bliss

From The Soil...

The hot, sunny Sri Lankan climate means that many of our ingredients grow all year round. Seasonal ingredients are harvested and left to dry in the sun before being put into airtight containers. This ensures all ingredients are as fresh and vibrant as the day they are picked.

While many of us recognise the cigar-shaped quills of cinnamon, the vibrant yellow of turmeric and the spicy warmth of cloves, our suppliers work with these ingredients from seed. Understanding the diverse range of soil types and varying temperature conditions, they work in harmony with the environment. From rich, fertile soil, our suppliers sow, grow and nurture robust crops to ripen and dry. From first contact to the last, our produce is handled with care and respect, ensuring delicate flavours are preserved.

Our pea flower tea and our spices are sold whole rather than ground, to maintain their freshest, strongest flavours and benefit from a longer shelf life. Our Curry Blends are blended using spice mixes from family recipes that have been passed down through generations of Sri Lankan families.

Our expertise in creating these blends ensures our Curry Blends are organic, authentic, original and quite simply, sensational.

To The Kitchen...

Sri Lankan kitchens are the heart of the home. As I relive my childhood memories, I am transported back to our family kitchen, with its jars of spices filling shelves and the sound of freshly picked herbs being ground, their aroma filling the house. Weekends brought a lively buzz of activity, with my sisters and I gathering fresh curry leaves, and my mum managing many bubbling pans. Bowlfuls of rice and curry were laid on the table to share with friends. Ensuring guests are comfortable is central to Sri Lankan hosting, and so my mum would stay in the kitchen, prepping the many dishes until few remaining morsels left meant our guests were full. This devotion, care and attention formed our cultural narrative, and a tradition I love to share.

Doors to Sri Lankan houses are always open, friends are welcomed and family are loved. Everyone is fed, and no one leaves with an empty stomach. As you recreate my recipes in your home, I hope you combine your own traditions with mine, and enjoy sharing delicious, wholesome food with your loved ones.

To the Plate

Traditional Sri Lankan meals consist of a bowl of rice placed in the middle of the table, with various curry dishes around it. All of my recipes and spices are designed with this in mind and allow you to create your very own Sri Lankan meals at home.

When I set up Rice's Bliss, I was committed to ensuring that other people like me, who value knowing the origin of their food have somewhere they can shop with confidence. If you care about what you eat, and where the food you cook comes from, you can rest assured that all of Rice's Bliss products are organic, free from artificial flavourings and additives, farmed naturally and packed with flavour.

Eating healthy, sustainable food, cooked from scratch doesn't need to be complicated. With a range of spices and flavours, you can create dishes to suit you. I love being able to support people as they learn to cook the Sri Lankan way, so am always on hand to answer any questions. If there's a particular recipe of flavour you've enjoyed, I'll be able to point you in the direction of other recipes you'll love. Regardless of your culinary skill and experience, you can learn to cook the Sri Lankan way. My recipe range starts with quick, simple dishes and when you've mastered the basics, the possibilities are endless.

A few tips about the ingredients I use

Curry Leaves:

Fresh curry leaves (Karapincha in Sinhala) are an essential ingredient in Sri Lankan cooking and have a distinctive, flavour and fragrance. I know that finding fresh curry leaves can be a challenge in most parts of the world.

I don't recommend using other herbs like bay leaves instead of curry leaves in Sri Lankan cooking. So, in my opinion, if you cannot find curry leaves, just skip them. Please remember that they are edible and have many health benefits, so you don't need to remove them.

If you don't use curry leaves daily, it can be a waste to buy a bunch of it from the shops or online. To save them longer, I suggest you wash and let them dry. Put them in an air-tight container or zip lock bag and freeze them. This way, you can keep your curry leaves around 6 months.

Green Chillies:

In Sri Lanka, green chillies are widely used as a cooking ingredient. They add a milder heat and enhance the flavour of the curries beyond just pure heat. You can skip them altogether if you don't like them or if you do not have them.

Green chillies can also be frozen: wash them, remove the stems, let them dry and freeze them in a zip lock bag or an air-tight container. They will last you over 3 months.

My favourite curry cooking oil:

Organic Coconut Oil is my favourite but you are welcome to use any vegetable oil like sunflower or olive.

Spices:

Most of the spices used in this recipe book can be found in most supermarkets but Sri Lankan Curry Blends are rarely found in shops and they are the most important ingredients in my recipes.

Here's what they are and where to find them.

Rice's Bliss Meat Curry Blend

Fourteen organic ingredients have been carefully dried and grounded together, then roasted to create a perfectly harmonious blend.

Rice's Bliss Unroasted Curry Blend

Found in every Sri Lankan kitchen, our unroasted curry blend is the base for many Sri Lankan vegetable and seafood curries.

Rice's Bliss Roasted Curry Blend

Dark roasted curry blend is used more for meat curries and some rare dishes like pineapple and jackfruit curries. Lightly roasted spice blends are popular in Sri Lanka but this dark roasted version is special. It's one of the ingredients that give Sri Lankan meat curries their amazing flavour.

Ground Black Pepper

Most Sri Lankans like to use chilli powder in vegetable curries but in many of my recipes you will see that I like to use black pepper. The reason for this is that chilli powder takes away the beautiful colours of certain vegetables, like green beans.

You can find Sri Lankan Meat Curry Blend, Unroasted Curry Blend, Roasted Curry Blend and many other spices at Rice's Bliss website:

www.RicesBliss.com

Contents

CHAPTER 1 : COOKING RICE — 22

Turmeric Rice — 24

CHAPTER 2 : VEGAN RECIPES — 26

Red Lentil Curry (Dhal) With Or Without Spinach — 28

Young Jackfruit Curry — 30

Okra Curry — 32

Cashew Nut Curry (w/ green peas & carrots) — 34

Pineapple Curry — 36

Devilled Potato — 40

Mung Bean Curry — 42

Mushroom Stir-Fry — 44

Coconut Sambol (relish) — 46

Beetroot Curry — 48

Green Bean Curry — 50

Carrot Stir-Fry — 52

Banana Pepper Curry — 54

Fried Aubergine Curry — 56

CHAPTER 3 : MEAT & SEAFOOD RECIPES 58

Chicken Curry 60

Devilled Chicken 62

Beef Curry 64

Pork Curry 68

Lamb (Mutton) Curry 70

Tuna Fish Curry 72

Monk Fish Curry 74

Devilled Prawns 76

Prawn Curry 78

CHAPTER 4 : TEA TO ACCOMPANY YOUR RICE & CURRY 80

Blue Butterfly Tea 82

CHAPTER 1

Cooking Rice

The central feature of Sri Lankan cuisine is the rice, so let's get that right first.

Here are few tips to cook your perfect rice:

- Wash the rice a few times till the water runs clear. This helps remove impurities and also reduces the starch content that can make your rice sticky.

- Add the water to commence cooking. I generally use 1 ½ cups of water to 1 cup of rice. Make sure you use the same measuring cup for both items. This can differ from the type of rice you use so make sure you read the label and follow instructions from there for the water.

- If using a pot/pan instead of the rice cooker, use a heavy bottomed pan with a good lid so that the rice cooks evenly. The size of the pot has to be suitable to the quantity of rice being cooked.

- Once done, allow the rice to sit for 5-10 minutes (do not open lid) and then fluff the rice gently (I use a chopstick). If you stir hot rice, it can break apart.

Chapter 1 : Cooking Rice

TURMERIC RICE

About the Recipe:

As this golden rice cooks, your kitchen will be filled with the fruity-sweet aroma of spices like cardamom and cinnamon. Turmeric rice is how many Sri Lankans celebrate anything from a birthday to a wedding.

A tip for the rice: rinse it thoroughly in cold water until the water runs clear, and leave for the excess water to drain away. This allows the coconut oil to really coat each grain.

INGREDIENTS

315g of white basmati rice

2 tbsp of coconut oil or butter

1 red onion, finely chopped

1 tsp black whole peppercorns

5-7 fresh curry leaves

1 tsp ground turmeric

5 whole cloves

5 cardamom pods, crushed open

1-2 inches of cinnamon stick split open by hand

50ml water + amount of water recommended on rice pack

100ml coconut milk

1 tsp of salt (or to taste)

Ingredients for garnishing

50g cashew nuts

30g raisins

½ onion sliced thinly, fried in a little bit of butter

INSTRUCTIONS

- Rinse the rice thoroughly in cold water until the water runs clear, and leave for the excess water to drain away.
- Fry the onions in a tiny bit of butter and set aside. (Optional)
- Heat the butter/coconut oil in a wok or a sauce pan
- Add cinnamon, curry leaves, cloves, cardamom & peppercorns
- Fry over a medium heat without burning the spices
- Add onion and sauté until the onion is golden brown
- Add the coconut milk along with the water
- Add turmeric & salt
- Boil the mixture for 1-2 minutes
- Add the washed rice with water (around 3 cups but double check instructions on pack)
- Lower the heat and cook for 15 to 20 minutes
- Remove from the heat and set aside

Garnishing

- In a small pan, fry the cashew nuts and raisins with 1 tsp of butter/coconut oil
- Garnish the rice with fried onions, cashew nuts & raisins
- Serve warm with a curry (or two) of your choice

Simple Modern Sri Lankan Cooking

Chapter 1 : Cooking Rice

In Sinhala, we call cooked rice: "Bath".

CHAPTER 2

Vegan Recipes

Sri Lanka is one of the most vegetarian and vegan friendly countries in the world. Their food is a celebration of fresh fruit and vegetables.

RED LENTIL CURRY (DHAL) WITH OR WITHOUT SPINACH

About the Recipe:

This dhal curry recipe is an authentic Sri Lankan recipe and can be cooked in under 30 minutes. Dhal is a popular and regular vegan side dish in most homes and restaurants.

Dhal and spinach is another popular quick vegan curry you can try for a healthier meal plan.

Cooked using red lentils, a few tempering ingredients, spinach and coconut milk, this creamy spinach and dhal curry makes a perfect budget-friendly side dish for your meals.

It's a quick, time-saving, versatile dish that can be served at any meal.

INGREDIENTS

250g washed red lentils

200g washed spinach (optional)

200ml coconut milk

6 fresh curry leaves

2 broken pieces of cinnamon sticks

1 tsp chilli flakes

1 red onion sliced

3 chopped garlic cloves

2/3 tsp turmeric

1 tsp chilli powder (more or less depending on your taste)

1 sliced green chilli with seeds

2 tsp Sri Lankan unroasted curry blend

1 ½ cups of water

½ tsp of salt (or to taste)

Tempering Ingredients (Optional)

1 tbsp coconut oil

1/4 red onion sliced

1 tsp mustard seeds

4-5 curry leaves

½ tsp chilli flakes

INSTRUCTIONS

- Make sure you have washed the lentils thoroughly. (This helps when cooking)
- Add the washed lentils to a pan.
- Pour in the water with the turmeric, curry blend, chilli flakes, chilli powder, onion, garlic, green chilli, cinnamon sticks and curry leaves.
- Over a high heat, let the water boil.
- When the water is boiling, turn the heat to medium, close with lid and let the lentils cook. (This usually takes 10-15 minutes)
- When the lentils are cooked (there should be no orange colour left, all should be yellow), add the spinach and cook for a further 5 minutes. This is optional.
- Gradually add the coconut milk and let it simmer on low heat. Stir every few minutes. (otherwise the coconut milk won't melt properly)
- Add salt to taste. (Do not add salt any sooner as the lentils won't cook properly)
- Serve warm with rice.

Tempering (optional but even nicer)

- In a non-stick pan, heat the oil and add onion, mustard seeds and curry leaves. Cook until the mustard seeds start to splutter. Add red chilli flakes if using and fry the mixture for a few seconds.
- Pour the tempering onto the cooked dhal & mix. (If I'm serving this to friends, I leave it on top and mix it just before serving.)
- Leftover dhal can be kept in the fridge in a covered container for up to 3 days or you can freeze it for up to 6 months.

In Sinhala, we call dhal: "Parippu".

Chapter 2 : Vegan Recipes

YOUNG JACKFRUIT CURRY

About the Recipe:

This Sri Lankan Jackfruit Curry is packed with so much flavour, you won't even realise it's meatless! This curry is perfect for vegetarians, vegans, and gluten free diets, or anyone who loves a good curry.

Here I'm sharing my mum's authentic Sri Lankan jackfruit curry recipe, using canned young jackfruit (obviously, my mum used the fresh "polos" picked straight from a tree in our garden!)

INGREDIENTS

400g of young jackfruit drained (I use biona)	½ tsp of chilli powder (less for a milder curry)
1 tbsp coconut oil	½ tsp of turmeric
1 red onion sliced	1 tsp ground cinnamon
2 garlic cloves chopped finely	1 tsp tamarind concentrate
8 fresh curry leaves	1 tsp of sugar (I use coconut sugar)
1 sliced green chilli with seeds	½ tsp of salt (or to taste)
2 tbsp of Sri Lankan roasted curry blend	¼ cup of water
½ tsp of ground black pepper (less for a milder curry)	¾ cup of coconut milk (full fat coconut milk would be best)

INSTRUCTIONS

- In a medium sized saucepan, heat the coconut oil over medium heat.
- When the oil is heated, add the onion, and sauté until softened.
- Add the garlic and sauté for a few minutes, but make sure not to let them burn.
- Add the curry leaves and let them fry in the oil for just a few seconds.
- Add the green chillies, curry blend, chilli powder, turmeric, black pepper, and ground cinnamon, and sauté the mixture for about 1 – 2 minutes to mix. The spices should be very fragrant, but again, make sure not to let them burn. Adjust the heat accordingly.
- Next, add the tamarind, salt, sugar, young jackfruit and mix to coat the jackfruit in the spice mix.
- Add the water and coconut milk and stir to mix. Increase the heat to medium high and bring the curry to a boil.
- Lower the heat to medium low, and let the curry gently simmer (with the lid slightly off) for about 45 minutes. If too much liquid is evaporating while cooking, add some water as needed.
- The jackfruit pieces should be nice and soft (check by pricking the "nose" of a jackfruit piece to see how easily it can be pierced with a knife/fork or skewer). Taste and season with salt to taste.
- After the curry has simmered and the jackfruit is soft, you can cook the curry uncovered for a few more minutes IF you prefer a thicker curry gravy. If the gravy is too thick for your liking however, add a little water. (I personally prefer a thicker gravy).
- Serve the curry warm with rice. But as with any curry, they do taste even better the following day! (This is definitely a dish I cook the night before when I serve it to guests).

In Sinhala, we call young jackfruit "Polos"

Chapter 2 : Vegan Recipes

OKRA CURRY

About the Recipe:

I always cook this dish with fresh okra (also known as ladies fingers in Sri Lanka) and plump juicy cherry tomatoes.

I love the freshness and simplicity of this dish; the flavours are delicate and it's not too heavily spiced.

INGREDIENTS

400g okra (prepared as explained below)

15 cherry tomatoes (sliced in half)

1 big red onion (thinly sliced)

4 thinly chopped garlic cloves

1 sliced green chilli with seeds

8 fresh curry leaves

½ tsp of turmeric

1/3 tsp chilli powder

1/3 tsp chilli flakes

1/3 tsp Sri Lankan unroasted curry blend

3 tbsp of coconut oil

1/2 cup of coconut milk

½ tsp of salt (or to taste)

pinch of sugar (optional)

INSTRUCTIONS

Prepare the okra:

- Rinse the okra thoroughly under cold running water.
- Rub spines off older, larger pods under running water. Okra pods begin to grow small, fuzzy spines as they mature that you need to remove before eating them. Hold any such pods under running water and gently rub them all over with a scouring pad, vegetable brush, or paper towel to remove the tiny spines.
- Pat the okra dry with a paper towel and leave it to air dry completely.
- Trim off the very tip of the stem with a knife and cut each okra into 3cm pieces.

Cooking:

Do not close the pan at any point during the cooking of this curry.

- Put the prepared okra into a bowl and add half of the onions, half of the garlic, green chilli, half of the curry leaves, chilli powder, turmeric, curry blend & salt. Mix and set aside.
- Heat a pan with the coconut oil. Once hot, add the remaining garlic, onion & curry leaves.
- When you can start smelling the garlic and it's starting to turn golden add the chilli flakes & mix.
- Now add the okra mixture to the pan along with a tiny pinch of sugar (this helps preserve the colour of the okra).
- When the okra is half cooked (about 5 minutes), add the coconut milk and the tomatoes. Cook a further 5 minutes or so without the lid.
- Serve with rice. (If you need to put the lid on, wait until it's completely cooled down.)

Chapter 2 : Vegan Recipes

In Sinhala, we call Okra "Bandakka"

Chapter 2 : Vegan Recipes

CASHEW NUT CURRY (W/ GREEN PEAS & CARROTS)

About the Recipe:

This creamy, mellow cashew curry is often the one soothing element—besides rice, of course—in an otherwise fiery Sri Lankan meal.

This traditional Sri Lankan Cashew curry has extra ingredients including green peas, carrots and other spices.

This is most probably the best Vegan recipe by far.

Cashews have many health benefits and this curry tastes amazing!

INGREDIENTS

150g of cashews (soaked & boiled, see below)

100g of carrots (diced into 1cm cubes)

100g of green frozen peas

1 red onion (thinly sliced)

1 green chilli (sliced)

4 cloves of garlic (chopped finely)

5 to 6 curry leaves

2 medium pieces of cinnamon or ½ tsp of ground cinnamon

½ tsp turmeric

¾ tsp chilli powder

1/3 tsp Sri Lankan unroasted curry blend

3 tbsp water

1 tbsp coconut oil

½ tsp tsp of salt (or to taste)

1 cup of coconut milk

Prepare the cashews:

Leave the unsalted raw cashew nuts soak in cold water for 2 to 3 hours.

Boil the cashews for 10 to 15 minutes until they get soft. I use the pressure cooker for about 2 minutes.

Drain and set aside

Simple Modern Sri Lankan Cooking

INSTRUCTIONS

- Heat a pan with the coconut oil in. Once hot, add half of the garlic. After a few seconds, add half of the curry leaves, half of the onions and half of the green chillies. Let it all fry for a few minutes.
- Now add the diced carrots, mix well and add 2 to 3 tbsp of water along with all the remaining garlic, half of the remaining onion, chillies, turmeric, cinnamon, chilli powder, unroasted curry blend, salt and let it cook uncovered. You should still have a bit of the onion and curry leaves left.
- Once the carrots have softened, add the green peas.
- Now add the coconut milk and let it warm up.
- Finally add the cashews and let it all cook for about 6 to 8 minutes. (without the lid).
- Now add the remaining onion & curry leaves and mix well. Adding these two ingredients at this stage will give you extra aroma and taste to this beautiful curry. Be gentle with the cashews, you do not want to break them.
- Once the milk has gone down and the cashews are cooked to your taste you can add some extra coconut milk if you would like some gravy, then cook a few more minutes on low heat uncovered and keep stirring every couple of minutes.
- Serve with rice.

In Sinhala, we call Cashews "Kaju".

Chapter 2 : Vegan Recipes

PINEAPPLE CURRY

About the Recipe:

If you are looking for a savoury pineapple recipe your family will love, then this easy 30-minute curry recipe should do it.

With all that natural sweetness and acidity in pineapple, you'll expect the pineapple curry recipe to retain the same flavours but it doesn't.

When it's cooked, this low carb Pineapple dish loses its natural sweetness and acidity making it a great side-dish for meat and seafood.

The fruit almost tastes like another vegetable dish that can certainly make a great accompaniment for your meatless meals as well.

INGREDIENTS

1 medium pineapple (Avoid pineapple that is too yellow near the crown or at the bottom. it's always safer to buy a greener pineapple, bring it home and let it ripen for a day and then use it.) Cut the pineapple as seen below (including the core)

1 red onion thinly sliced

3 chopped garlic cloves

2 tsp of sugar (I use coconut sugar)

½ tsp of ground cinnamon

½ tsp of ground cloves

1 sliced green chilli with seeds

8 fresh curry leaves

1 tsp mustard seeds

1 tsp of chilli powder (more or less depending on your taste)

2 tsp of Sri Lankan roasted curry blend

½ tsp of turmeric

½ cup of coconut milk

2 tbsp of coconut oil

3 tsp of salt (or to taste)

Simple Modern Sri Lankan Cooking

INSTRUCTIONS

- Heat a wok then add the coconut oil.
- When the oil is hot, add the mustard seeds and wait until you hear them pop.
- Now add turmeric, ground cinnamon, ground cloves and salt to season.
- Add garlic, onion, green chilli & curry leaves and sauté for a few minutes until the onions have softened.
- Add chilli powder. It will start to turn darker in colour; wait until you can smell the spices.
- Now add the roasted curry blend.
- Add the pineapple with the sugar and mix everything together. 
- Cook covered for about 20 minutes.
- Add the coconut milk. 
- Cook uncovered for another 5 minutes or until the gravy has gone down to your liking.
- Serve with rice.

Chapter 2 : Vegan Recipes

38

Chapter 2 : Vegan Recipes

In Sinhala, we call Pineapple "Annassi".

Chapter 2 : Vegan Recipes

DEVILLED POTATO

About the Recipe:

This devilled potato curry can be enjoyed with any of your favourite curry combinations.

It really is a spicy potato fry recipe, full of taste compared to any other regular curried potato recipes I know.

Feel free to adjust the spices; you can easily adjust the heat of this potato curry by reducing the amount of chilli flakes used.

This dish really goes well with any carbs, rice, coconut flat bread

INGREDIENTS

250g potatoes (peeled and sliced into roughly 3cm pieces)

1 to 2 big red onions (thinly sliced) If you like onions, you can add a lot of it to this recipe.

4 garlic cloves (thinly chopped)

2 sliced green chillies with seeds

8 fresh curry leaves

1 tsp of turmeric

½ tsp chilli powder

½ tsp chilli flakes

1 piece cinnamon stick

3 tbsp of coconut oil

½ tsp of salt (or to taste)

INSTRUCTIONS

- Put your potato pieces into a large saucepan with the salt and turmeric and bring to the boil. Cook for around 10 minutes, until they're just starting to become tender, then drain.

- Heat the coconut oil in a large frying-pan and add in the garlic, then the sliced onions & cinnamon stick. Stir-fry over a medium heat until they soften and turn translucent.

- Next, pop in your curry leaves, chilli powder, chilli flakes, green chillies and a pinch of salt.

- Add your cooked potatoes and mix gently until coated. Fry for a few more minutes until the surface of the potatoes is golden brown. (Be gentle not to break the potatoes and smash them too much.)

- Serve with freshly cooked rice and your favourite curries.

Simple Modern Sri Lankan Cooking

Chapter 2 : Vegan Recipes

In Sinhala, we call Potatoes "Ala".

Chapter 2 : Vegan Recipes

MUNG BEAN CURRY

About the Recipe:

Mung beans are rich in vitamins and minerals. These beans are one of the best plant-based sources of protein.

Mung Bean Curry is well known for its healthy & delicious credentials like its 'bean cousin' red lentil curry. It's all about soft nutty taste of mung beans along with coconut milk & other lovely spicy ingredients. Mung Bean Curry is a popular choice of day to day Sri Lankan cooking.

INGREDIENTS

- 1 cup of mung beans (pre-soaked in water for at least 3 hours)
- 1 cup of water
- 1 red onion thinly sliced
- 4 chopped garlic cloves
- 2 sliced green chillies with seeds
- 8 fresh curry leaves
- ½ tsp mustard seeds
- 3 broken pieces of cinnamon
- 1 tsp of chilli powder (more or less depending on your taste)
- 2 tsp – Sri Lankan unroasted curry blend
- ½ tsp of turmeric
- 2 tbsp of coconut oil
- 1 cup of coconut milk
- ½ tsp of salt (or to taste)

INSTRUCTIONS

- In a bowl, soak the mung beans overnight or at least for 3 to 4 hours.
- Drain the excess water and put mung beans in a sauce pan and add water, half of the onion, 2 garlic cloves, 4 curry leaves, curry blend, chilli powder, turmeric, green chilli, cinnamon and salt.
- Mix well all together and keep cooking until mung beans are boiled for about 10 minutes.
- Now pour the coconut milk into the saucepan & cook for further 10 minutes in low medium heat.
- Transfer the mung beans into a separate bowl.
- Add the coconut oil into the same saucepan. When oil is hot add mustard seeds and fry for about 2 minutes until mustard seeds are popping.
- Now add the remaining half of the onion, garlic and curry leaves into the sauce pan and fry it for a few minutes on medium heat.
- When onions are golden, add mung beans into the sauce pan and mix well.
- Adjust salt to your taste.
- Remove from the heat and serve with rice.

In Sinhala, we call Mung Beans "Mung Ata".

Chapter 2 : Vegan Recipes

MUSHROOM STIR-FRY

About the Recipe:

In Sri Lanka, oyster mushrooms are very popular. This mushroom stir-fry recipe will allow you to add those vegetarian proteins to your meal. Mushrooms are a great vegetarian protein that you can add to your meals.

INGREDIENTS

200g oyster mushrooms torn into thin strips

1 red onion thinly sliced

3 chopped garlic cloves

2 sliced green chillies with seeds

1 medium tomato sliced

8 fresh curry leaves

1 tsp mustard seeds

½ tsp of ground cinnamon or 3 broken pieces of cinnamon sticks

1 tsp of chilli flakes (more or less depending on your taste)

1 tsp of ground black pepper

½ tsp of turmeric

2 tbsp of coconut oil

½ tsp of salt (or to taste)

INSTRUCTIONS

Prepare the mushrooms:

- Tear the mushrooms into thin strips and wash. Gently squeeze the water out and put the mushrooms into a bowl.
- Mix the mushrooms and tomatoes with salt, pepper and turmeric and leave to the side.

Instructions

- Heat a wok with the oil.
- When the oil is hot add the mustard seeds and wait until you hear them pop.
- Add the garlic and let it get golden.
- Now add onions, curry leaves and green chillies, cinnamon and fry until the onions soften on low heat.
- Now add the mushrooms/tomato mix and cook until the mushrooms are soft. (This shouldn't take more than 4 to 5 minutes)
- Add the chilli flakes and cook for another minute.
- Check taste and add salt if needed.
- Serve with rice.

Simple Modern Sri Lankan Cooking

Chapter 2 : Vegan Recipes

In Sinhala, we call Mushrooms "Bim Mal".

Chapter 2 : Vegan Recipes

COCONUT SAMBOL (RELISH)

About the Recipe:

Coconut sambol is one of the well-known dishes among Sri Lankans. People prepare this dish very often for breakfast, lunch, or dinner. The coconut sambol is the best combination with every food, especially with Sri Lankan bread.

This easy coconut sambol is one of the easiest recipes you can make quickly at home.

Sri Lanka is the world's 4th largest coconut producing nation! Not only do they export a large quantity of coconut (in various forms) but it is also a staple in the Sri Lankan diet, or a food (grated coconut, oil or coconut milk) used in cooking.

The shells are made into bowls and spoons amongst other things like the buttons on our packaging. I for one love using my coconut spoons when serving.

INGREDIENTS

1 fresh whole coconut (grated) or 100-150g desiccated coconut

½ lime juice

1 medium tomato finely diced and de-seeded

1 medium red onion or 3 shallots finely sliced

1 tsp chilli flakes

½ tsp chilli powder

½ tsp of salt (or to taste)

1 green chilli chopped (optional)

INSTRUCTIONS

- Prepare all your ingredients.
- Place the coconut, tomato, onion, chilli flakes and chilli powder in a bowl and mix thoroughly. I mix it by hand (using a food glove) because I find it blends better that way. But a spoon will do too.
- Add half of the lime juice and some salt to taste and mix again.
- Then add the green chilli pieces (if using). Mix well.
- The sambol should be moist and reddish in colour from the chilli powder. Taste test and add more lime and salt if needed.
- Mix again and serve with rice or bread.

Top Tips

You can remove the seeds from the fresh chilli for a slightly less chilli taste. You can also cut the green chillies into bigger pieces so you can pick them out when eating.

If using desiccated coconut, soak it in a little bit of hot water or hot coconut milk (I mix with a bit of both) to re-hydrate it.

Simple Modern Sri Lankan Cooking

Chapter 2 : Vegan Recipes

In Sinhala, we call Coconut "Pol".

Chapter 2 : Vegan Recipes

BEETROOT CURRY

About the Recipe:

This Beetroot Curry is a comforting dish that pairs well with steamed rice and other side dishes.

Beetroots are commonly grown in the hill country in the central part of Sri Lanka. They are a popular "super-food" with plenty of nutritional value.

The key to perfect beetroot curry is simple. Don't overcook the beetroot. If it gets soggy, it'll lose quite a bit of it's delicious potential.

Prepare the beetroot:

Prepping and cutting the beetroot is the hardest part. Making the beetroot curry is the easiest. Since the beetroot is cooked in coconut milk, the resulting curry gravy is creamy, sweet, with a touch of spice (you can adjust the heat to your liking), and it's also got that gorgeous deep pink/red colour!

First wash the beetroot.

Slice the tops and peel them.

Slice the beetroot, halve the slices and cut into batons.

Ingredients

500g of beetroot (about 2 large, washed, peeled & cut)

½ red onion finely sliced

2 green chillies sliced

2 cloves of garlic chopped finely

6 curry leaves

1 tsp of Sri Lankan unroasted curry blend

¼ tsp turmeric

½ tsp chilli powder

¼ tsp of salt (or to taste)

½ cup of coconut milk (more if you like a thick gravy)

½ cup of water (more if you like a thin gravy

Simple Modern Sri Lankan Cooking

INSTRUCTIONS

- Place the cut beetroot in a saucepan (see above on how to cut the beetroot, trust me how you cut it MATTERS), along with the onions, sliced green chilli, garlic, curry leaves, unroasted curry blend, turmeric powder, chilli powder and salt. Mix well to combine.

- Stir in the coconut milk and water.
- Heat the saucepan over medium high heat, while stirring occasionally, until the coconut milk/water comes to a boil.
- Reduce the heat to a simmer, and let it cook covered, for about 5 minutes.
- Uncover and cook for a further 5 – 10 minutes while stirring frequently, until the beetroot is cooked to al dente (cooked through but not soggy). The cooking time will vary depending on the thickness and sizes of the beetroot.
- If the liquid is evaporating too quickly, you can add more water or coconut milk.
- Taste and add more salt if necessary.
- Serve with rice.

In Sinhala, we call Beetroot "Rathu Ala".

Chapter 2 : Vegan Recipes

GREEN BEAN CURRY

About the Recipe:

Young fresh fine green beans are a joy. Sri Lankan Green Bean Curry is a traditional recipe, which inevitably has many versions. I'd like to share with you mine which is actually my mum's recipe. She truly is the most amazing cook. Most of my recipes are inspired by her.

INGREDIENTS

400g green beans (topped, tailed and cut into 3 then halved)

1 big red onion thinly sliced

4 chopped garlic cloves

1 sliced green chilli with seeds

8 fresh curry leaves

½ tsp of ground cinnamon

1 tsp of ground black pepper (more or less depending on your taste) Most Sri Lankans like to use chilli powder but we like to use black pepper as the chilli powder takes away that beautiful green colour of the beans.

2 tsp Sri Lankan unroasted curry blend

½ tsp of turmeric

2 tbsp of coconut oil

½ cup of coconut milk mixed with ½ cup of water

¼ cup of thick coconut milk

½ tsp of salt (or to taste)

INSTRUCTIONS

- In a bowl, mix the beans with cinnamon, ground pepper, turmeric, unroasted curry blend and salt. Leave to one side.
- Heat a pan with coconut oil.
- Once the oil is hot, add the garlic and fry for a few seconds. Don't let it burn.
- Now add the onions, and curry leaves. Lastly add the green chilli. Fry for a few minutes until the garlic turn golden and onions are soft.
- Now add the beans, mix well.
- Add the coconut milk mixed with water. Cook for about 5 to 10 minutes, uncovered until the beans are cooked to your taste. Give it a stir every few minutes.
- When the beans are cooked, add the thick coconut milk. This will give you a nice thick gravy. Cook for another 2 to 3 minutes. If you feel like there's too much gravy, cook a little longer.
- Remove from the heat and serve with rice and another curry or two.

Chapter 2 : Vegan Recipes

In Sinhala, we call Beans "Bonchi".

Chapter 2 : Vegan Recipes

CARROT STIR-FRY

About the Recipe:

This is an easy to make, mouth-watering and a colourful recipe. Delicious with rice and a chicken curry or another veg curry like green bean curry or a dhal curry.

INGREDIENTS

4 to 5 medium size carrots (cut thinly, thinner the better)

1 big red onion finely sliced

4 chopped garlic cloves

1 sliced green chilli with seeds

8 fresh curry leaves

½ tsp of ground cinnamon

1 tsp of ground black pepper (more or less depending on your taste) Most Sri Lankans like to use chilli powder but I like to use black pepper as the chilli powder takes away that beautiful colour of the carrots.

½ tsp of turmeric

3 tbsp of coconut oil

½ tsp of salt (or to taste)

INSTRUCTIONS

- In a bowl, mix the carrots with ground black pepper, turmeric and salt. Leave to one side.
- Heat a pan (I prefer a wok) with the coconut oil.
- Once the oil is hot, add the garlic and fry for a few seconds. Don't let it burn.
- Now add the onions and curry leaves. Lastly add the green chilli. Fry for a few minutes until the garlic turn golden and onions are soft.
- Now add the cinnamon and mix all together.
- Finally add the carrots and mix all together. Do not cover.
- Stir every few minutes and let it all fry for about 5 to 8 minutes.
- Serve warm with rice and any other curry of your choice.

Simple Modern Sri Lankan Cooking

Chapter 2 : Vegan Recipes

Here's an easy one.
In Sinhala, we call Carrot "Carrot".

Chapter 2 : Vegan Recipes

BANANA PEPPER CURRY

About the Recipe:

Banana peppers are also known as yellow wax pepper or banana chilli.

This dish is so simple, yet one of my favourites.

I love the freshness and simplicity of this dish; the flavours are delicate.

You can choose to take the seeds out for a milder curry but I think the seeds are what make this curry special.

INGREDIENTS

400g banana peppers (cut into halves, or into 5cm pieces)

15 cherry tomatoes sliced in half

1 big red onion finely sliced

4 thinly chopped garlic cloves

1 sliced green chilli with seeds

8 fresh curry leaves

½ tsp of turmeric

1/3 tsp chilli powder

1/3 tsp chilli flakes

1/3 tsp Sri Lankan unroasted curry blend

3 tbsp of coconut oil

½ cup of coconut milk

½ tsp of salt (or to taste)

INSTRUCTIONS

Do not close the pan at any point during the cooking of this curry.

- Put the prepared banana peppers into a bowl and add half of the onions, half of the garlic, green chilli, half of the curry leaves, chilli powder, unroasted curry blend turmeric & salt. Mix and set aside.

- Heat a pan with the coconut oil. Once hot, add the remaining garlic, onion & curry leaves.

- When you can start smelling the garlic and it's starting to turn golden add the chilli flakes & mix.

- Now add the banana peppers mixture to the pan.

- When the banana peppers are half cooked (about 5 minutes), add the coconut milk and the tomatoes. Cook a further 5 minutes.

- Serve with rice. (If you need to close the curry, wait until it's cooled down.)

Chapter 2 : Vegan Recipes

In Sinhala, we call Banana Pepper "Maalu Miris".

Chapter 2 : Vegan Recipes

FRIED AUBERGINE CURRY

About the Recipe:

This Sri Lankan fried aubergine curry is a savoury and sweet heaven with just the right balance of flavours. It is one of the best dishes my mum makes and anyone that tastes this curry falls in love with it instantly.

And most of all I like to use my air fryer to fry the aubergine to make it healthier but do feel free to deep-fry yours (after all, that's how my mum made it).

Tips about Air frying aubergine and making the curry:

- Do it in small batches. Only fill the air fryer basket in one layer. So there's enough space for the air to circulate and that ensures even frying and browning.
- Make sure you shake the basket halfway through. Again for even frying.
- Do not wash your aubergines after you cut them. You can wash them before you fry them. But if you wash them after you cut them, it would take too long for the aubergines to fry and could make them soggy too.
- Do not mix salt when you fry them. Salt would draw the water out of the aubergines pieces and would make them soggy.
- Make sure every piece of aubergine is coated with oil before you put them into the basket.
- Air fried aubergines need a little more time to get the desired tenderness than deep-fried aubergines. So make sure you cook it in low heat, so aubergines can absorb all that deliciousness from the curry and rehydrate.

INGREDIENTS

To air-fry aubergine (can be deep-fried too)

350 grams Aubergine (I prefer the baby aubergines but not a must)

½ tsp turmeric powder

1 tbsp coconut oil

To make the curry

¼ cup finely chopped onion

2 small green chillies (or to your spice level)

3 garlic cloves chopped

6 to 8 curry leaves

2 tsp Sri Lankan roasted curry blend

1 tsp sugar (I use coconut sugar)

1 tsp tamarind

1 tsp of salt (or to taste)

1 tbsp coconut oil (less if you make with deep-fried aubergine)

½ cup thick coconut milk

¼ cup water

Simple Modern Sri Lankan Cooking

INSTRUCTIONS

First, let's prepare and air-fry (or deep fry) the aubergine.

Cut the cleaned aubergines into two-inch-long cylindrical pieces. And then cut each cylindrical piece into halves. Then cut each half into 4 - 6 wedges depending on the thickness of the aubergines.

As soon as you finish cutting your aubergines, mix in your turmeric, salt and oil with the aubergine pieces. This will help prevent the aubergine from changing colour and going brown. If you're deep-frying, no need to mix oil, just mix your turmeric & salt.

Put them into the air fryer basket and arrange them into one layer (with the given amount you may have to air-fry them in two-three batches depending on the size of your air-fryer) and fry for 7 - 10 mins on 200C. Make sure to shake the basket a few times to ensure even frying.

Making the curry

- Heat a pan, add the coconut oil and let it heat up. Then add the curry leaves. Let them splatter. Add chopped garlic, chopped onion, sliced green chillies and let them fry a little.
- Now add the roasted curry blend, sugar, salt, and tamarind. Sauté a few seconds to mix everything in.
- Then add your air-fried/deep-fried aubergine and mix well. The spices should coat every piece of aubergine.
- Now add your coconut milk and water and let the curry come to a simmer.
- Taste and see if it needs any more salt or sugar and adjust accordingly.
- Cook uncovered on low heat until the aubergine rehydrates, the curry thickens up and you get the desired amount of gravy. This curry is better as a dry curry so I usually dry up the curry until there is only a little bit of gravy left. And when the pan cools down it thickens up even more.
- Serve with rice and another dish of your choice.

In Sinhala, we call Aubergine "Batu".

CHAPTER 3

Meat & Seafood Recipes

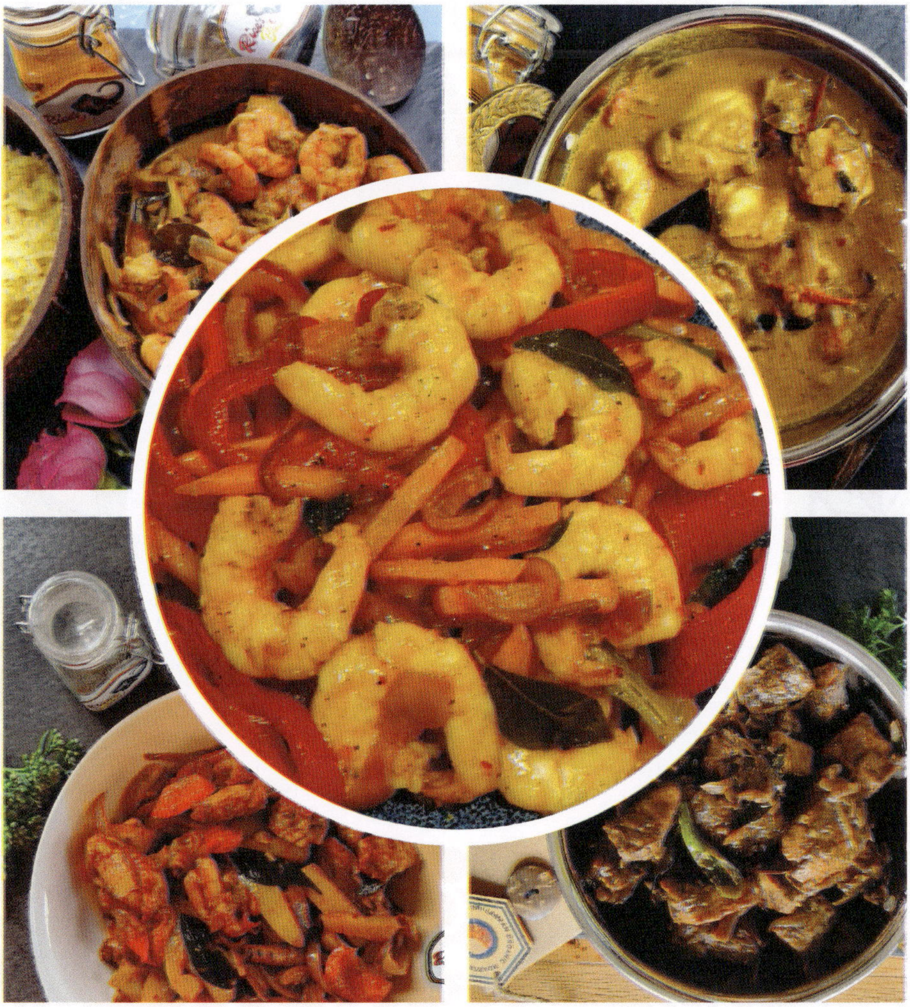

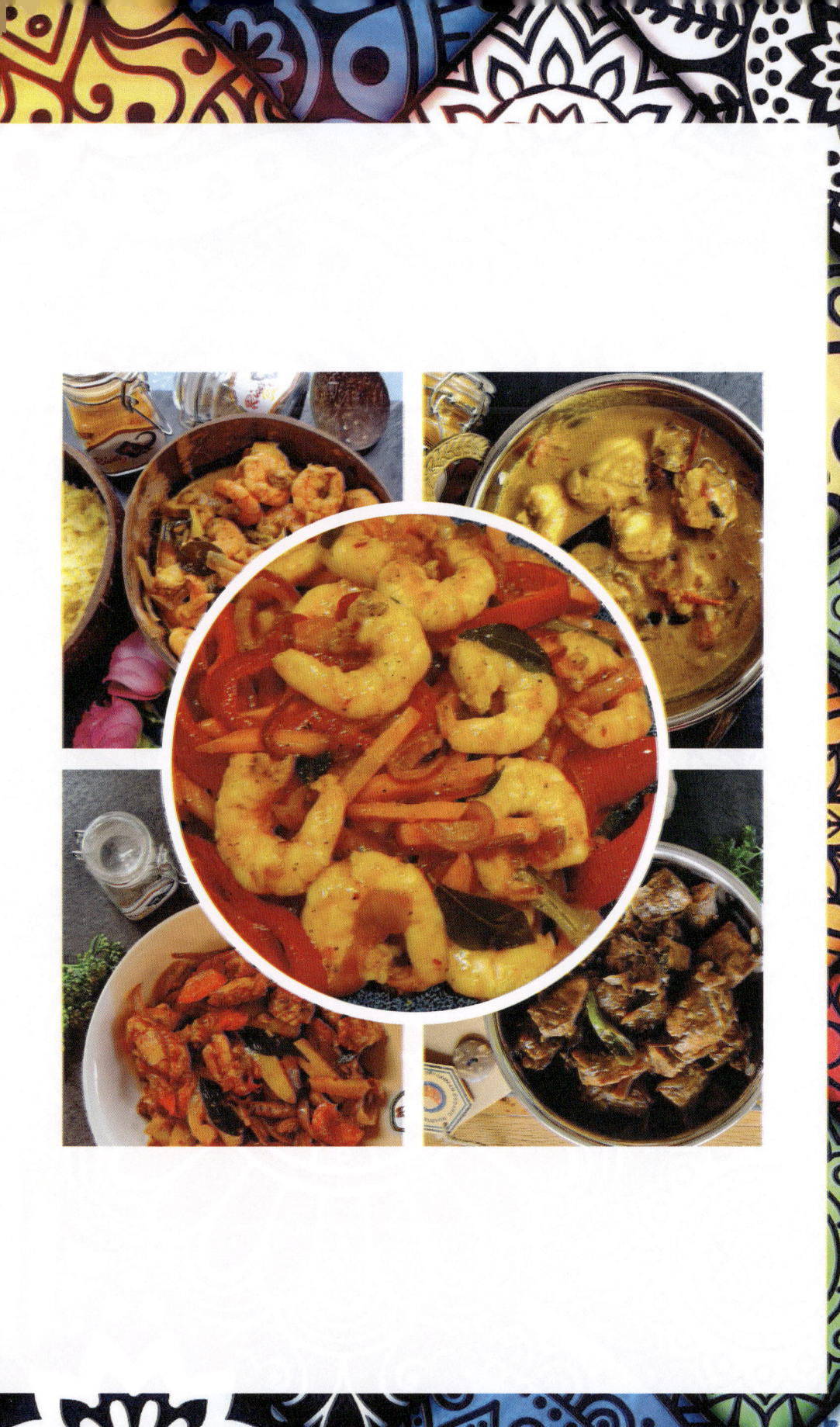

Chapter 3 : Meat & Seafood Recipes

CHICKEN CURRY

INGREDIENTS

1 kg of chicken (whole chicken cut into sections or any boned chicken thigh or leg pieces (large thigh pieces should be cut in half))

3 tbsp coconut oil

1 red onion sliced

4 garlic cloves chopped

8 fresh curry leaves.

2 tbsp Sri Lankan meat curry blend

2 tsp Sri Lankan roasted curry blend

½ tsp turmeric

1-2 tsp of chilli powder

1 big piece of cinnamon stick or 1 tsp ground cinnamon

1 tsp ground cloves

1 tsp of salt (or to taste)

½ tsp ground black pepper

2 sliced green chillies with seeds

2 medium sized tomatoes cut into cubes OR 2 tbsp tomato puree

½ cup of water

About the Recipe:

This Sri Lankan Chicken Curry that we call "Kukul Mas" Curry in Sinhala is a must whenever I make a curry. It's also comfort food for my husband and I and we are instantly reminded of Sri Lanka, of my childhood, of home, of full and comforting meals, every time we eat this Sri Lankan chicken curry.

If you're new to the world of curries, or even if you are a pro, this curry is a must try! I often make this with dhal and serve with rice.

You can make this chicken curry with boned pieces from a whole chicken, or just boned pieces of just chicken legs or chicken thighs. Or for convenience, you can just use boneless pieces of chicken. Obviously, boneless chicken will cook faster, and is my choice when I want to cook a quick curry that can be ready in less than 30 minutes. BUT, a GOOD chicken curry uses boned chicken pieces because the bones flavour the gravy.

If you're using boneless chicken, I recommend using the brown meat over white meat of chicken. Chicken thighs (brown meat) has more flavour and won't overcook easily and can withstand the cooking time.

For a healthier option you can use sliced boneless chicken breasts too. But make sure to cook them for a shorter amount of time OR braise them for a longer time to make it tender. Otherwise the pieces will be too dry.

> In Sinhala, we call Chicken "Kukul Mas". "Mas" is meat.

Simple Modern Sri Lankan Cooking

INSTRUCTIONS

- Marinate the chicken with the meat curry blend, roasted curry blend, black pepper and salt. Leave to the side. (You can leave this overnight in the fridge or just a few hours or even just 10 minutes. Up to you.)

- Add the coconut oil into a large saucepan and heat the oil over medium heat. Add onion and garlic to the heated oil and cook until softened.

- Add cinnamon, cloves, turmeric, curry leaves, green chillies and chilli powder; mix to combine. Cook for a few minutes until you start to smell the spices.

- Add the chicken, tomatoes (or tomato puree) and mix to coat. Cook for 10 minutes with the lid off, on medium high heat. Stir frequently to make sure the chicken or the spices don't burn.

- Add water and bring the curry to a boil. If you want less gravy, add less liquid. (Sometimes, I don't add any water)

- Lower the heat and let it simmer with the lid closed for about 20 minutes, stirring occasionally. The chicken should be completely cooked by this point. Taste the curry and season to taste. You can add more salt if needed.

- If the chicken curry gravy is too thin, or there's too much of it, uncover and simmer the curry for a further 10 minutes or longer. This step is optional, but it will allow the water to evaporate and the gravy to thicken.

- Turn off the heat and let the chicken cool down slightly.

- Serve with rice and a dhal curry.

Chapter 3 : Meat & Seafood Recipes

DEVILLED CHICKEN

About the Recipe:

Despite how spicy the dish is, once you've tasted a bowl of chicken devil, you'll be wanting to take the next bite of the Sri Lankan style chilli chicken. It's a popular restaurant menu dish that anyone visiting the country to explore or visiting family, seem to remember. Once you learn to make the devil chicken dish, I'll guarantee, you'll be making it as often as possible.

A bowl of quick & easy fried rice makes a great accompaniment for this chicken dish. I use an air-fryer to fry the chicken (to make it healthier) but you can also shallow fry it until the chicken turns slightly crispy. This is a simple enough dish you can create at home with ingredients you can easily find in the kitchen.

INGREDIENTS

500g chicken pieces (I prefer boned chicken pieces but I'll leave that up to you)

2 tbsp coconut oil

1 tsp turmeric

½ tsp chilli powder

1 tsp ground black pepper

½ tsp chilli flakes

5 fresh curry leaves

2 broken pieces of cinnamon sticks or ½ tsp of ground cinnamon

2 large red onions cut into wedges

2 chopped garlic cloves

3 medium sized tomatoes cut into wedges

4 banana peppers sliced or red & yellow peppers

2 tbsp oyster sauce

2 tbsp soy sauce

4 tbsp tomato sauce

1 tsp of salt (or to taste)

INSTRUCTIONS

- Place the chicken pieces in a bowl.
- Add turmeric, chilli powder, black pepper, half of the coconut oil (if using an air-fryer) & salt. Combine and set aside for around 15 minutes.
- After 15 minutes, fry the chicken in the air-fryer or heat half of the coconut oil and shallow fry the chicken until they turn golden brown on the edges. You might need to fry the chicken a bit at a time.
- Heat the remaining oil in the same pan. Add the garlic & cinnamon, let it fry a little and add the onion, curry leaves & banana peppers. Sauté until the onions and peppers slightly soften.
- Now add the tomatoes and sauté for a few more minutes.
- Pour in the tomato sauce, soy sauce, oyster sauce and chilli flakes.
- Combine and cook over medium heat for around 5 minutes.
- Once the onion and peppers have softened, add the chicken to the pan and cook for another 2 minutes over medium heat. Cook until the sauce is thick and completely coats the chicken with a little gravy left.
- If you find the curry too spicy, you can add a little bit of sugar at the end.
- Serve warm with a quick & easy fried-rice or even on its own as a side dish. This is a perfect dish to accompany your aperitif.

In Sinhala, we call Meat "Mas".

BEEF CURRY

About the Recipe

The beauty of this Sri Lankan beef curry is that it's just so earthy, tender and the spices are balanced to perfection. I have also simplified this recipe like all recipes in this book to make it an everyday dish.

Use a cut of beef that doesn't need to be simmered for too long – like sirloin. You can use chuck as well, but cut it into thin slices, instead of bite-sized pieces. Make sure the sirloin is also cut into thinner pieces, since this will also help with keeping the meat tender, and cook the curry faster.

INGREDIENTS

Beef Marinade

600g beef chuck or sirloin cut into small pieces

3 tsp Sri Lankan roasted curry blend

2 tsp of salt (or to taste)

Curry

2 tbsp coconut oil

1 big red onion sliced

6 garlic cloves finely chopped

2 green chillies sliced

1 inch ginger minced

8 curry leaves

1 tsp Sri Lankan meat curry blend

1 tsp Sri Lankan unroasted curry blend

1 tsp ground black pepper (less for a milder curry)

1 tsp chilli powder (less for a milder curry)

1 tsp ground cinnamon

½ cup of water

½ cup of coconut milk

more salt to taste

INSTRUCTIONS

- Add the beef pieces into a bowl with the marinade ingredients, Sri Lankan Roasted curry blend and salt. Mix well and leave overnight in the fridge or just an hour or two outside.
- If left in the fridge overnight, bring the meat to room temperature before cooking.
- Heat a large pan over medium high heat. Add the oil, and once heated, add the onion and sauté for a few minutes until the onions start to soften.
- Add the garlic, ginger, curry leaves, and green chillies. Sauté until the onions are translucent.
- Add the unroasted curry blend, meat curry blend and sauté for a few seconds until you can smell the spices.
- Now add the rest of the spices, along with the marinated beef. Stir well to coat the beef with the spices.
- Sauté the beef for about 5 minutes in high heat. Let the meat caramelize while giving it a good stir every now and then.

- Add the water and let it come to a boil.
- Now add the coconut milk and stir well.
- Lower the heat to a simmer. Let the curry simmer uncovered, for about 30 minutes. Stir regularly.
- Add a little more water, if needed. If the water is evaporating too much, you can also place the lid on the pan half way through the cooking time.
- When the meat is very tender, about 30 to 40 minutes, the curry is ready.
- Let the curry preferably rest for about 30 minutes to let the flavours mingle and serve with rice.

Chapter 3 : Meat & Seafood Recipes

In Sinhala, we call Beef "Harak Mas". "Mas" is meat

Chapter 3 : Meat & Seafood Recipes

Chapter 3 : Meat & Seafood Recipes

PORK CURRY

About the Recipe

This pork curry is cooked in aromatic spices on a low heat for a long time until it melts in your mouth. Try this curry once and you're going to think of this curry every time you see a piece of pork.

INGREDIENTS

Pork Marinade

600g pork (I recommend loin chops) cut into 1 inch cubes

1 tsp ground black pepper

3 tsp Sri Lankan roasted curry blend

½ tsp ground cinnamon or 3 broken pieces of cinnamon

½ tsp chilli powder

1 tsp tamarind paste

1 tsp of salt (or to taste)

Curry

2 tbsp coconut oil

2 green chillies sliced

1 inch ginger minced or sliced

4 garlic cloves sliced

1 red onion sliced

8 curry leaves

1 tsp sugar (optional)

1 cup of boiled water (more or less depending on how much gravy you would like)

More salt to taste

Simple Modern Sri Lankan Cooking

INSTRUCTIONS

- Add the pork pieces into a bowl. Keep bones and a bit of the meat fat as this will add extra flavour to your curry.
- Add all of the marinade ingredients to the meat, Ground Black Pepper, Sri Lankan roasted curry blend, ground cinnamon or broken pieces of cinnamon, chilli powder, tamarind paste and salt. Mix well and leave overnight in the fridge or just an hour or two outside.
- If left in the fridge overnight, bring the meat to room temperature before cooking.
- Heat the oil in a saucepan over medium heat. When the oil is hot, add the curry leaves, ginger and onions and sauté till the onions become translucent. Add the garlic and sliced green chillies and sauté for another couple of minutes.
- Add the marinated pork and sugar and mix well. Add the water and bring this to boil.
- Lower the heat to medium-low and let it simmer for about 45 minutes. Keep an eye on the curry and add extra water if the curry dries out or you would like more gravy.
- Taste and add extra salt if needed.
- You can serve this curry straight away or leave it a few hours; it'll taste even better.

In Sinhala, we call Pork "Uru Mas". "Mas" is meat

Chapter 3 : Meat & Seafood Recipes

LAMB (MUTTON) CURRY

About the Recipe:

There seems to be some confusion between lamb and mutton. Some Asian countries like Sri Lanka & India call lamb, mutton. Some other countries seem to call goat meat and sheep's meat, lamb.

So to be clear this recipe is for goat or sheep's meat.

INGREDIENTS

Lamb Marinade

250g lamb (cut into small chunks)

1 tbsp Sri Lankan meat curry blend

1 tbsp Sri Lankan roasted curry blend

1 tsp of ground black pepper (more or less depending on your taste)

½ tsp of turmeric

½ tsp tamarind concentrate

2 tsp of salt (or to taste)

Curry

1 red onion finely sliced

5 garlic cloves chopped

1 tsp chilli powder (adjust to your taste)

10 fresh curry leaves

1 green chilli sliced

2 pieces 6 cm cinnamon stick or ½ tsp of ground Cinnamon

¼ tsp of ground cloves

1 cup of water

2 tbsp of coconut oil

½ cup of coconut milk (optional)

More salt to taste

INSTRUCTIONS

- In a bowl, mix the lamb and all the marinade ingredients (meat curry blend, roasted curry blend, black pepper, turmeric, tamarind and salt) and keep it aside. (You can leave this in the fridge overnight or just a few minutes to couple of hours outside. The longer, the better.)

- Heat the coconut oil in a pan. I like to use a clay pot for this curry but a wok or a pan is fine.

- When the oil is hot, add the onion and fry for a minute.

- Now add the garlic, curry leaves and green chillies and fry for another couple of minutes while mixing.

- Then add ground cloves, cinnamon and the chilli powder and mix well to combine with the onions.

- Now add the marinated lamb and fry for 5-6 minutes in high heat. At this stage you might need to add a little extra coconut oil, especially if you are using a lean piece of lamb.

- Reduce the heat to medium and add the water, mix the curry and let it all cook for about 15 minutes.

- When the curry is boiling OR when the water level is ½ way down, you can add coconut milk (if you wish) and keep it on heat for another 10-15 minutes.

- If you like a thick curry, cook for a little longer.

- Serve the curry warm with rice or coconut flat bread. But as with any curry, they do taste even better the following day! (This is definitely a dish I cook the night before when I serve it to guests)

Simple Modern Sri Lankan Cooking

Chapter 3 : Meat & Seafood Recipes

In Sinhala, we call Lamb "Batalu Mas".

Chapter 3 : Meat & Seafood Recipes

TUNA FISH CURRY

About the Recipe

I am sharing here with you a Sri Lankan-style spicy tuna fish curry recipe. It is a great way to incorporate tuna or any other firm fish (sword fish, sailfish…) into a curry.

Sri Lankan fish curry is legendary and that's no surprise, considering Sri Lanka is an island in the heart of the Indian Ocean. I grew up eating a lot of fish, in a lot of different ways. Fried fish was my favourite way of eating fish as a kid, but now as an adult, I've come to appreciate the incredibly complex flavours that this simple and aromatic fish curry has to offer!

INGREDIENTS

Tuna Marinade

500g tuna cut into 1 inch cubes

½ tsp ground black pepper

1 tsp Sri Lankan roasted curry blend

¼ tsp turmeric

½ tsp chilli powder

1 tsp of salt (or to taste)

Curry

1 red onion finely sliced

5 garlic cloves chopped

1 inch of ginger minced

10 fresh curry leaves

2 green chillies sliced

2 tsp Sri Lankan roasted curry blend

1-2 tsp of chilli powder (adjust to your taste)

½ tsp ground black pepper (this is optional if you'd prefer a milder curry)

2 pieces 6 cm cinnamon stick or ½ tsp of ground cinnamon

½ tsp turmeric

1 tsp tamarind concentrate

2 tbsp coconut oil

2 cups of thick coconut milk (optional)

more salt to taste

INSTRUCTIONS

- Place the fish in a bowl, along with all the marinade spices. Mix to coat and let the fish marinate for 10 – 20 minutes.
- While the fish is marinating, prep and start to cook the curry.
- Heat the coconut oil in a pan.
- When the oil is hot, add the onion and sauté until it starts to soften.
- Then add the garlic and ginger, and sauté until the onion has further softened.
- Add the curry leaves, green chillies, turmeric, roasted curry blend, black pepper, chilli powder and cinnamon. Sauté for about a minute until the spices become fragrant, but take care not to let them burn.
- Now add the fish and tamarind, and gently mix until the fish is coated with all the spices.
- Add the coconut milk and stir it in. This step is optional; you can just make it without and have a dry fish curry or you can add water for a spicier, thin gravy curry.
- Bring the curry to a boil over medium heat. Then lower the heat to a gentle simmer, and simmer the curry without the lid for about 20 minutes or until the fish is cooked through.
- Taste and add more salt and/or tamarind to taste.
- Let the curry sit for at least 10 – 20 minutes if you can, before serving. This allows the flavours to develop further. Leftovers taste even better!
- Serve the fish curry with rice and other curries.

In Sinhala, we call Tuna "Kelawalla".

Chapter 3 : Meat & Seafood Recipes

MONK FISH CURRY

About the Recipe:

This simple fish curry is prepared with ingredients that are almost always found in Sri Lankan kitchens and is excellent served with steamed rice.

You can use virtually any white fish for this curry. My favourite is monk fish.

INGREDIENTS

250g white fish (I'm using monkfish for this recipe) cut into chunks

2 tbsp coconut oil

6 garlic cloves chopped

1 red onion finely chopped

1 medium tomato cut into wedges or 6 cherry tomatoes halved

8 curry leaves

1 sliced green chilli with seeds

1 tsp of chilli powder (more or less depending on your taste)

½ tsp of turmeric

2 tsp of Sri Lankan unroasted curry blend

1 piece of 4cm cinnamon or ½ tsp of ground cinnamon

¾ cup of coconut milk

¼ cup of water

Few drops of lemon juice to season (optional)

1 tsp of salt (or to taste)

INSTRUCTIONS

- Heat a pan over medium high heat and add the coconut oil.
- Once the oil is hot, add curry leaves, onion, green chillies, garlic, cinnamon, turmeric and let it all fry until fragrant.
- Now add curry blend and chilli powder and mix well for another minute or so.
- Add the tomatoes and mix everything together.
- Add the fish to the pan and mix gently.
- Add the water and coconut milk and cook until the fish is cooked. Let it simmer while gently stirring now and then. Do not close.
- Taste and season with salt and a few drops of lemon juice if needed.
- Serve with rice. Enjoy!

Chapter 3 : Meat & Seafood Recipes

In Sinhala, we call Fish "Malu".

Chapter 3 : Meat & Seafood Recipes

DEVILLED PRAWNS

About the Recipe:

Devilled prawns; a popular Sri Lankan prawn recipe for spicy seafood lovers. Served with plain white basmati rice, this dish is an absolute favourite in our household.

It's a simple enough dish you can create at home with ingredients you can easily find in the kitchen.

INGREDIENTS

400g raw jumbo king prawns

4 tbsp coconut oil

½ tsp turmeric

1 tsp chilli powder

½ tsp ground black pepper

1 tsp chilli flakes

8 fresh curry leaves

2 green chillies halved

10 cherry tomatoes halved

2 large red onions, halved then sliced (not too thin)

2 banana peppers sliced or 2 red long peppers sliced (you can also use red, orange or yellow bell peppers)

2 carrots sliced and cut into strips

4 tbsp tomato sauce (like Ketchup)

1 tsp of salt (or to taste)

INSTRUCTIONS

- Place the prawns in a bowl and add half of the turmeric, half of the ground black pepper and a pinch of salt. Mix well and leave to the side.

- Heat a wok or frying pan with the coconut oil. Now add the prawns and fry both sides until the prawns turn pink. This shouldn't take more than a couple of minutes. Do not overcook your prawns. Remove the prawns from the pan to a separate dish while you prepare the vegetables. Keep the remaining oil in the pan.

- To the remaining oil in the pan, add the onions and curry leaves and fry for a few minutes. When the onions start to soften, add the carrots, peppers and green chillies. Add the remaining ground black pepper, chilli powder, turmeric and a pinch of salt. Keep mixing for a few of minutes until the carrots are cooked to your liking. I like it crunchy in this recipe.

- Now add the prawns back with the cut tomatoes, chilli flakes and the tomato sauce. Mix well for another minute.

- Serve warm with plain white rice or even on its own as a side dish. A perfect dish to accompany your aperitif.

Chapter 3 : Meat & Seafood Recipes

In Sinhala, we call Prawns "Isso".

Chapter 3 : Meat & Seafood Recipes

PRAWN CURRY

About the Recipe

An easy recipe that can be adapted for any type of prawn or shrimp you have at hand. If you love a prawn curry, then I guarantee that this will be the best you've ever had! The full depth of flavour of this prawn curry comes from the whole prawn! And that includes the head of the prawn, especially the head. But the good news is that even if you can't find head-on prawns, it's OK! I've spent a lifetime eating prawn curry, made with peeled, unpeeled, head-on, headless etc., and it still tastes rich and flavourful.

INGREDIENTS

- 400g raw king prawns
- 2 tbsp coconut oil
- 6 garlic cloves chopped
- 1 red onion finely chopped
- 10 fresh curry leaves
- 1 sliced green chilli with seeds
- 1 tsp of chilli powder (more or less depending on your taste)
- ½ tsp of black pepper powder (less for a milder curry)
- ½ tsp of turmeric
- ½ tsp of Sri Lankan unroasted curry blend
- ½ tbsp tamarind concentrate
- ¾ cup of coconut milk (full fat coconut milk would be best)
- ¼ cup of water
- ½ tsp of salt (or to taste)

INSTRUCTIONS

- Put the prawns in a bowl and add the unroasted curry blend, turmeric, black pepper and salt. Mix and leave to marinate a few minutes.
- Heat a saucepan over medium high heat and add the coconut oil.
- Once the oil is hot, add half of the onions, half of garlic and half of curry leaves and sauté for a few minutes, but make sure not to let them burn.
- Now add the chilli powder with the green chilli and mix it all together.
- Now add the tamarind concentrate
- Pour the ¼ cup of water into the pan and mix.
- Now add the coconut milk and bring to boil while stirring.
- Finally add the prawns to the gravy base and mix gently.
- Cook about 10 minutes on medium to low heat until the prawns are cooked through and it is nice and pink. (Do not overcook or the prawns will feel like rubber)
- Taste and season with salt if needed.
- Serve with rice.

Simple Modern Sri Lankan Cooking

In Sinhala, we call Prawn Curry "Isso Maluwa".

CHAPTER 4

Tea to accompany your Rice & Curry

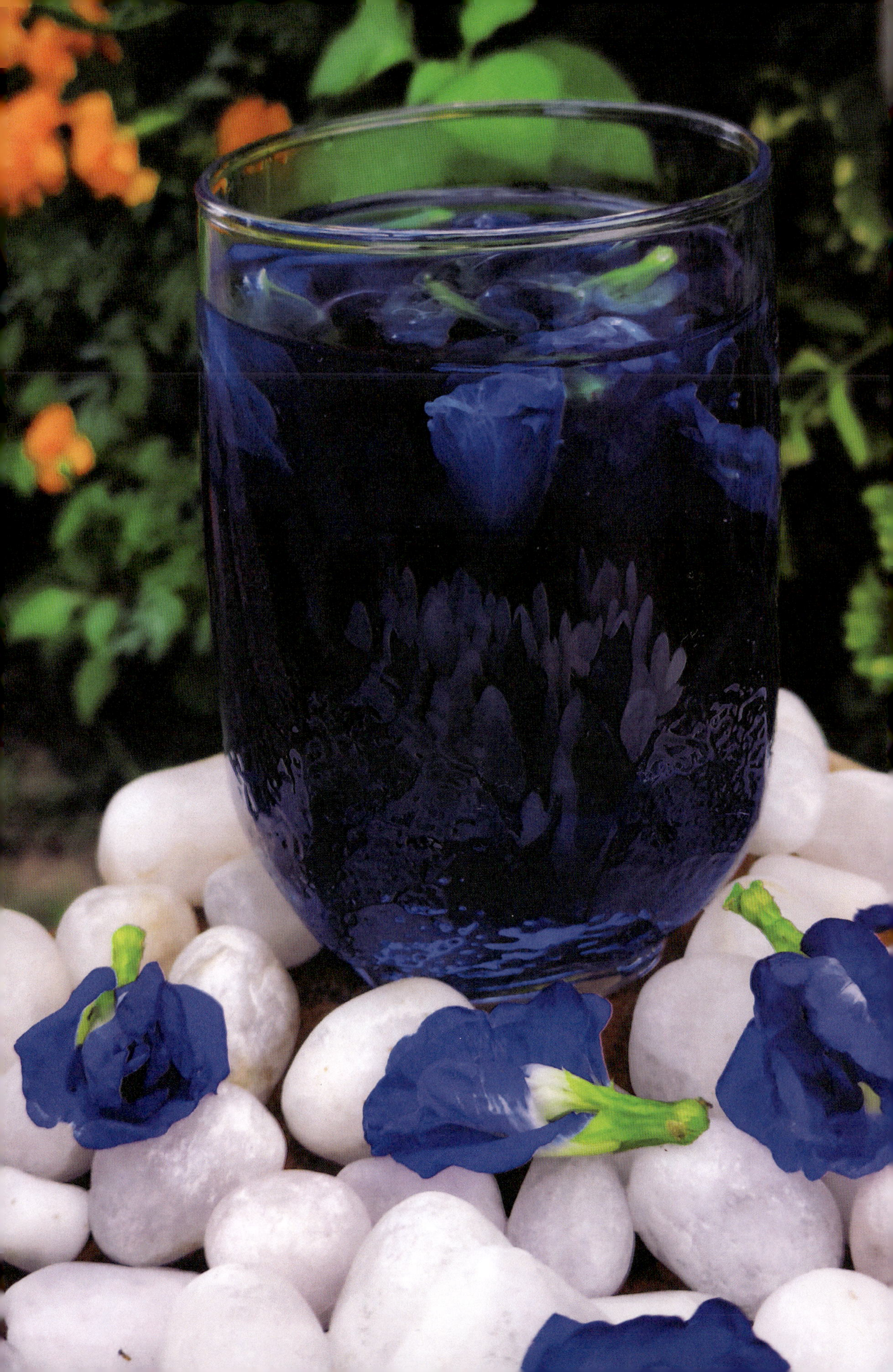

Chapter 4 : Tea to accompany your Rice & Curry

BLUE BUTTERFLY TEA

Also known by its scientific name, Clitoria Ternatea, the butterfly pea is a plant native to Asia, where it's praised for its health benefits in traditional Ayurvedic medicine. You may recognise it by its striking, vibrant blue flowers.

Often featured in cocktails, cosmetics, and herbal tea blends, butterfly pea flower is an ingredient well-known for its brilliant blue hue.

You may have heard about butterfly pea flower in health and diet circles. In recent years, the plant has also been studied for its antioxidant content and healthy properties.

In particular, some studies suggest that butterfly pea flower may help ensure skin and hair health, promote weight loss, and reduce blood sugar levels.

Growing up, my mum gave us this tea to help with tummy pain and indigestion.

Okay, time to put the kettle on and make this wonderful blue butterfly tea to accompany your rice & curries.

INGREDIENTS

1 tbsp dried butterfly pea flowers

1 slice of lemon (the lemon will turn the tea purple instead of blue, so if you want a blue colour, leave the lemon out but I like the taste of lemon in this tea)

1 thick piece of ginger chopped

coconut sugar, honey or your favourite sweetener to sweeten (optional)

hot water

INSTRUCTIONS

Depending on the amount of butterfly pea flowers you use to brew this drink, the tea will have different shades of blue.

If you add the lemon, it'll be more purple.

- Add all ingredients together in your favourite mug and pour hot water.
- Give a stir and let the flowers steep for 5 minutes.
- As time passes, you'll see the flowers release their blue pigments in hot water.
- Once ready, filter out the flowers and discard them.
- Serve the tea warm, sweetened to taste with raw honey, maple syrup, or a sugar-free sweetener. My favourite is organic coconut sugar.

Simple Modern Sri Lankan Cooking

Chapter 4 : Tea to accompany your Rice & Curry

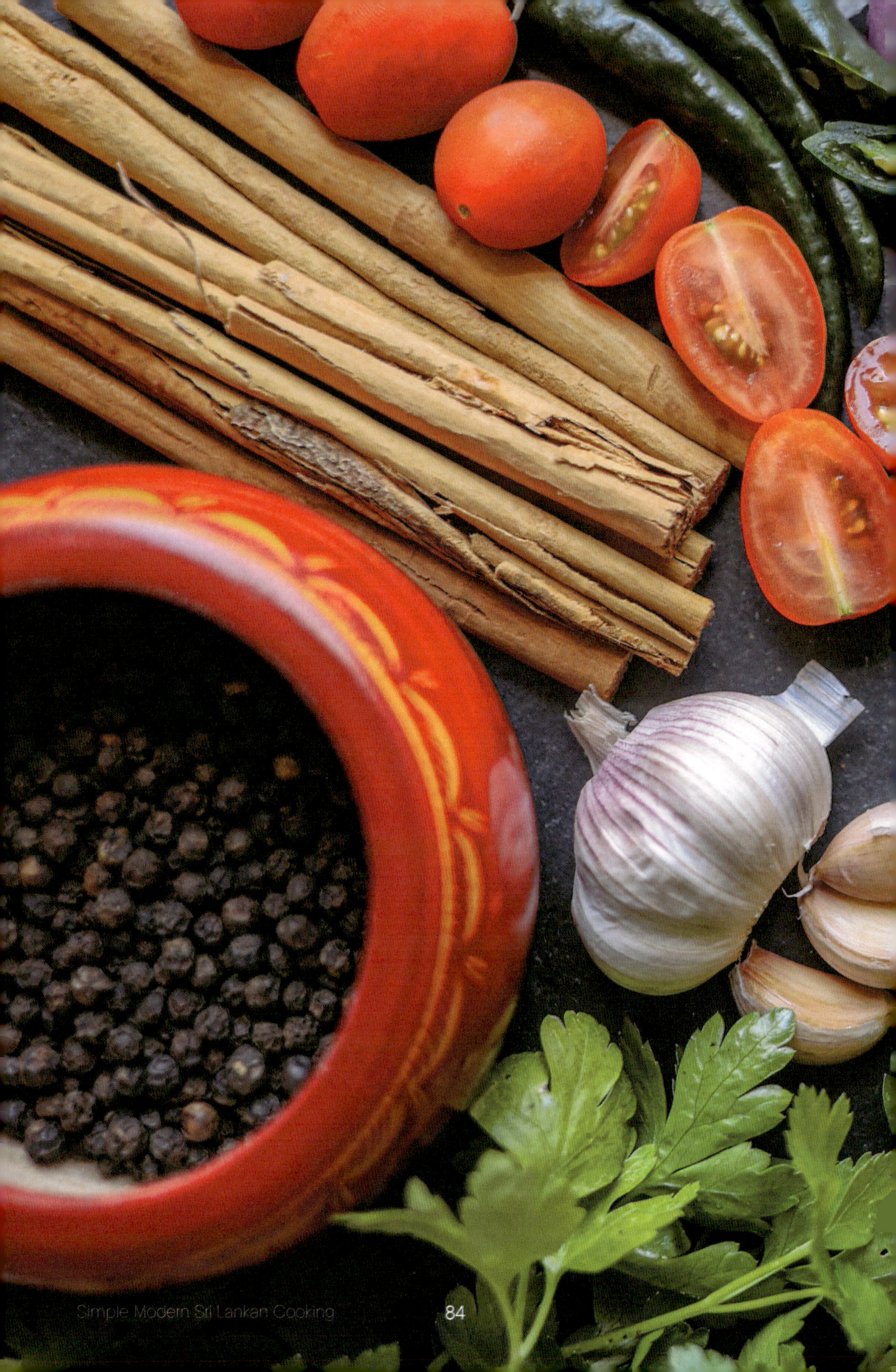

Get in touch

Here's how you can get in touch with Mahesha and Rice's Bliss:

- @MaheshaRice
- @RicesBliss
- @RicesBliss
- enquiries@ricesbliss.com
- www.RicesBliss.com

Share your creations on Social Media using hashtags **#MaheshasRecipes** and **#RicesBliss**

We would love to see them and share them with the world.

Thank You

This book is dedicated to my whole family.

My grandmother, Sudu Amma, for watching over me and giving me the strength to make my dreams a reality.

My dad, Appachchi, for teaching me to dream big and to never give up on my dreams.

My mum, Ammi, for embracing me with her love for cooking and for her confidence that I could achieve anything I wanted to.

My sisters, Thanusha & Iresha, for the incredible support through all my life, no matter the distance between us.

My adopted parents, Appachchi & Ammi, for opening the path for me to a bright future.

My parents-in-law, Mum & Dad, for their constant support and love.

My beautiful two children, Kayleigh & James for all the love that they show me daily.

Last but certainly not least, my amazing husband, Alistair for being my ROCK! Thank you for always believing in me and supporting me.

Thank you, all! I love you!

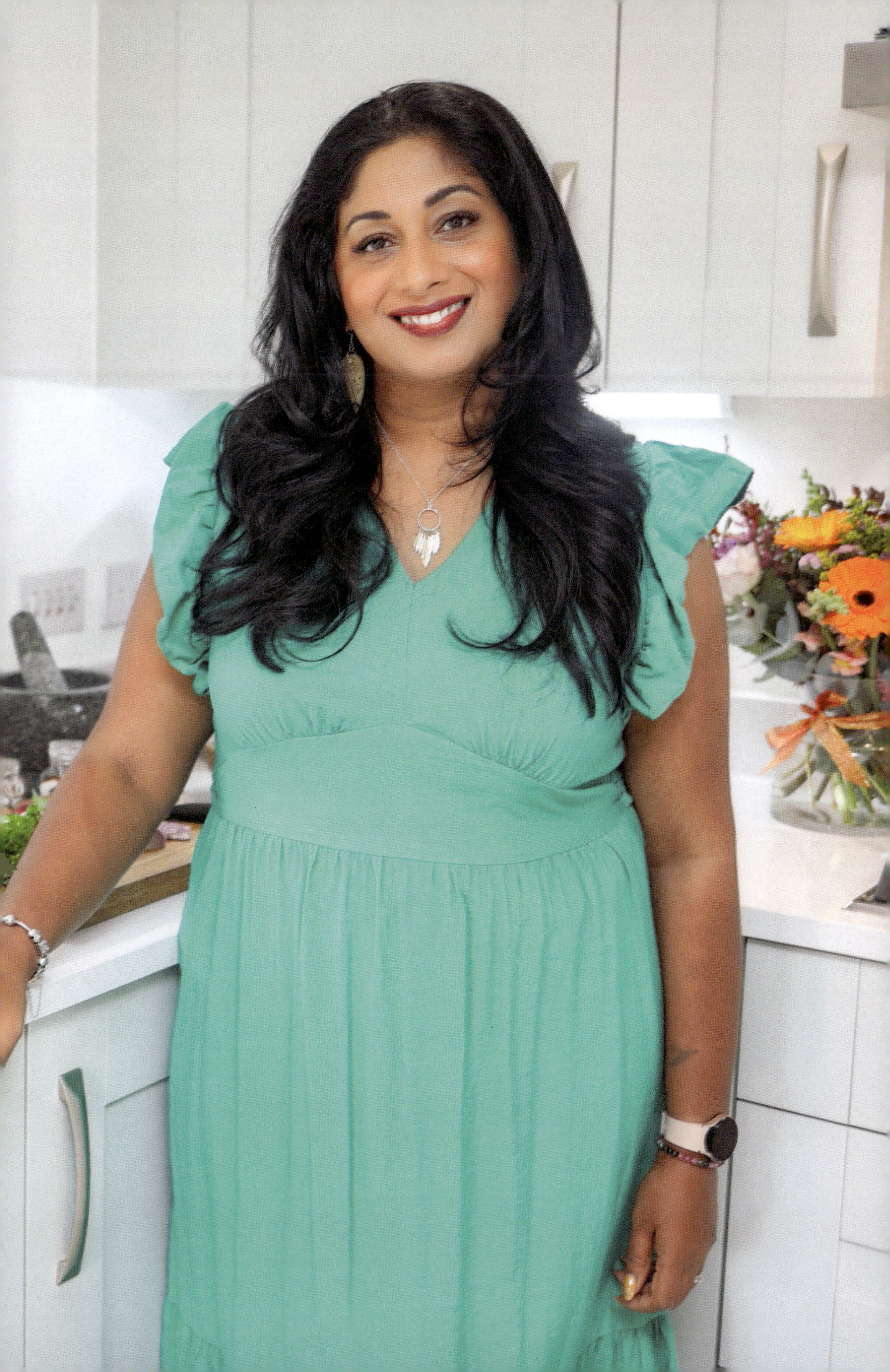

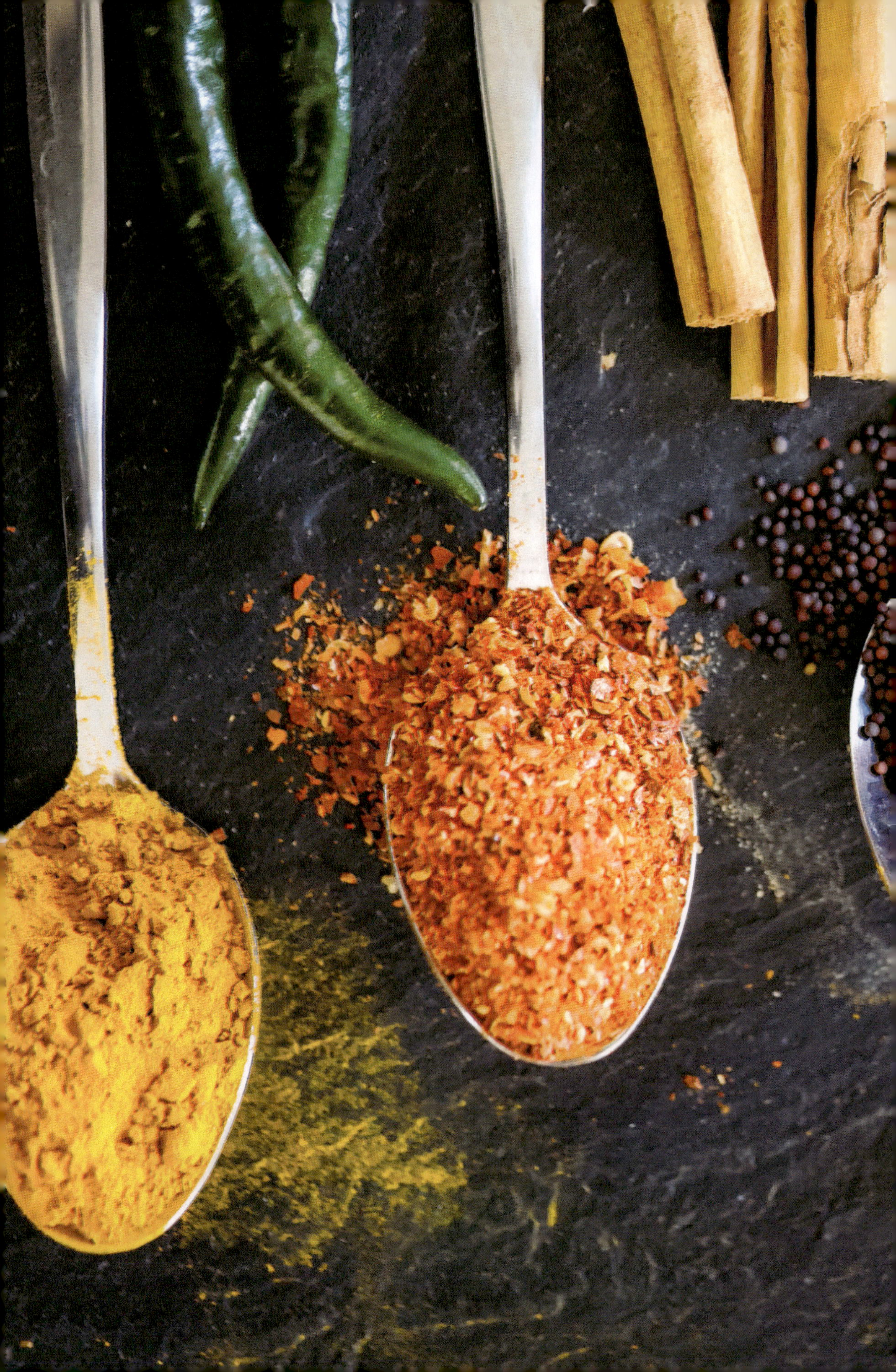

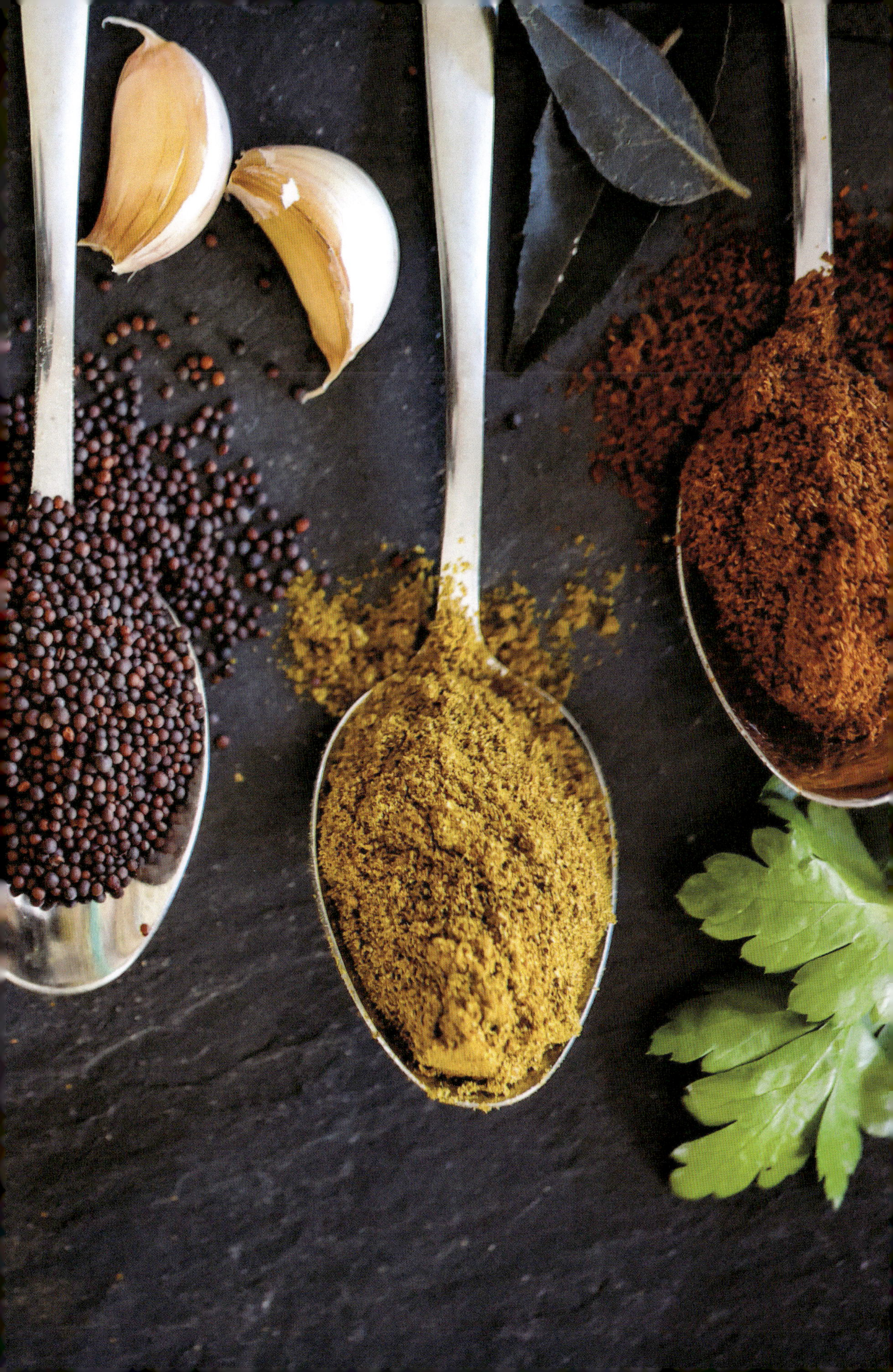

NOTES

NOTES

NOTES

NOTES

NOTES

NOTES

NOTES

NOTES

NOTES

NOTES

NOTES

NOTES

Printed in Great Britain
by Amazon